HUMAN/NATURE

poems by

LANCE LEE

PREVIOUS BOOKS

Poetry

BECOMING HUMAN

WRESTLING WITH THE ANGEL

Plays

TIME'S UP AND OTHER PLAYS

TIME'S UP

FOX, HOUND & HUNTRESS
in Vol. 10, PLAYWRIGHTS FOR TOMORROW

Novels

SECOND CHANCES

Non-Fiction

THE DEATH AND LIFE OF DRAMA
reflections on writing and human nature

ON THE WATERFRONT
(essays: contributor)

A POETICS FOR SCREENWRITERS

THE UNDERSTRUCTURE OF WRITING
FOR FILM AND TELEVISION
(WITH BEN BRADY)

ACKNOWLEDGMENTS

These poems have appeared, often in multiple issues, in "Panther in an Old Wood," *Acumen*; "Muskrat," "What A Man Gives," "Father Death,""Soft Weathers," *Agenda*; "Thin,""Play Within Plays," "Actaeon," "Rembrandt's Women," "My Best Friend,""Escape," "Hard Grace,""Eurydice;""Heron, Carmel;" "Passages," "The Owl," "Coyote," "Dreams Are," *Ambit* "Autumn," *Art Life*; "Why Jeffers Still Builds Tor Tower," "Harry's Place," *Blue Unicorn*; "The Owl" (short version), "The Dolphin," *Connecticut River Review*; "Harry's Place" (English edition), "Stonehenge in Winter" (English edition), *Manifold* "Idyll" "Hotel Dieu," "Winter Solstice," "Dreams," "Give Wing," *New Horizons*;"Kidnapped," "Live in the Lie of Love," *Orbis*; "Winter Gardens," "Against the Grain," *POEM* "Spring,""Buddha in Los Angeles," *Poetry Nottingham*; "Late Spring," "Orion Setting," *Quattrocentro*; "Haunting," *Scintilla* "Stonehenge in Winter (US),""Muskrat" (US), *Sow's Ear Poetry Review*;"The True Self is Not in Motion," *Solo*.

Copyright © 2006 by Lance Lee

All rights reserved. Except for brief passages in a review or article, no part of this book may be reproduced in any form or by any means without permission in writing from the publisher.

First edition
Library of Congress Control No.: 2006924865
ISBN: 9780913559994

Cover by John Robertson

Published by:
 Birch Brook Press
 PO Box 81
 Delhi, NY 13753

Write for free catalog of books and art.
Visit BBP at www.birchbrookpress.info
birchbrook@usadatanet.net

...to Jeanne

CONTENTS

I / From the Family Romance

Late Spring
    What A Man Gives/11
    My Father's Song/15
    Father Death/17
    Haunting/19
    By Love's Doing/21
    Virgin Spring/23
    Late Spring/24
    Soft Weathers/26
    Peace/28
Escape/29
Kidnapped/31
My Best Friend/32
Hard Grace/34
Anniversary Card/35
Live in the Lie of Love/37
Winter Gardens/38
Against The Grain/39

II / Passages

On The Beach At Quidnet/43
Passages/45
The Church at Ovingdean/47
Hotel-Dieu, November/50
The Death of a Sparrow/51
Plays Within Plays/52
Buddha in Los Angeles/54
Dreams/55

Why Jeffers Still Builds Tor Tower/56
Harry's Place/58
Aberfoyle/60
Hannibal / At Sixty/62
Crone/64
Actaeon/66
Eurydice/71
Rembrandt Talks About His Women To Me/74
Eros in Piccadilly/77

III / Through Nature

Thin. . ./81
Tracks/82
Idyll/84
Stonehenge in Winter/86
Winter Solstice/87
A Panther in an Old Wood/88
The Owl/89
Coyote/91
The Dolphin/93
Muskrat/95
Contraseasons
    Autumn/99
    Spring/101
    Summer/103
    Winter/106
Given Wing/109
Dreams Are/110
Heron, Carmel/112
Orion Setting/114
The True Self Is Not in Motion/116

About the Author/117
About the Book/119

I / From the Family Romance

LATE SPRING

poems on my father

What A Man Gives
My Father's Song
Father Death
Haunting
By Love's Doing
Virgin Spring
Late Spring
Soft Weathers
Peace

WHAT A MAN GIVES

    I

His heart explores its inward flaw,
his bone its wither; he is a leaf quivering
on the branch, a breath of air...

He frightened my youth,
a domineering, hostile man:
now I wonder if he will fall
as once he fainted into my arms
paying for lunch at Nate & Al's:

bills flapped in the air,
coins wheeled across the floor,

but he recovered and hurried off,
a street actor improvising for a later show
while the ambulance I called
ferried up Beverly Drive all siren,
turning each gray head...

    II

Sometimes he is a house
whose rooms are grieving old women
who draw black shawls tight,
for my sister and I rarely visit here—

some love-starved child in him

made him starve those he loved in turn:
now he goes room to room,
an old child wondering where
his sundered family has gone.

He was the son less loved
by a woman so foolish
she chose between twins: early and late,
their photos show him glowering
while his twin smiles smiles

smiles.

So he is doomed to be compressed
by love until he goes, for he fears
the more deeply love is held
the more certain love must fail.

   III

Mother tired of the women
he denied to her but regaled
to me. He split himself in two,
in three, in... and thought
he was faithful to mother's part.

Now, at lunch, young waitresses
dote on him, smiling
at his flattery; they see
the shadow of a ladies man,
while he swears me to lie

so his second wife younger

than his daughter won't know
we dine in regal elegance,
lamenting "The folly of
this marriage I endure

for fear the stress of breaking
it will break me too.
I've had bad luck in women,
I've loved unwisely. I suffer
from chronic heart chronic

skin disease— some days
I'm so tired it hurts to stand.
My career gives no solace,
devoted to ephemera:
the years are stones that grow

and bear me under."

    IV

When unleavened darkness rises
will he hear a song
that braids all half-measures,
failures and shames
into a larger harmony?
Or dream some wild gesture,

skydiving with no parachute
to grasp death in pure defiance
expansive, released,

for choosing makes free
whatever its end?

At last put to rest
the need to be first
that gene and early accident
conspired role by role
to make him miss,

and now give all he could
or would or should? No,
who does? He will whisper, if he can,
once there is no other choice,
or signal a final 'yes' to pull the plug,
and sink, emblematic to the end.

    V

I will mourn him long and hard
and hold my sheaf of sung defiances
to slow the fading of anger and love—
only accidents of time bring

virtues to light, and not faults
to condemn a man past recall:
only pride makes a man deny
all men are of a kind.

> *My heart explores its inward flaw,*
> *my bone its wither—I am a leaf quivering*
> *on the branch, a mere breath of air...*

MY FATHER'S SONG

My blood is singing
behind my right eye.
I am half blind with song.
From the left
the world lurches
me side to side.
Pains hound
across my chest after
what fox, what hare:
I feel their fear.
My right leg
declares its presence,
my right forearm aches
as though raked and torn—
suddenly I know
I am the goal
of fleet savage feet.
Is this a stroke descending?
Or am I feeling
the mortal state
my father feels
in his barren room,
ticking after the seconds
his eyes chase
around the clock?
We are less separate,
less I/Thou than we think.
My blood is singing

his song, and his? Note
by note he scales
towards that silence
I fear one day will be
all of song I hear.

FATHER DEATH

Twice I had to say "Yes, that's him"
first when my father died at the home
open-mouthed between breaths,
second at Mt. Sinai where a dwarf
wheeled him in silent and bloodless
as if stunned from seeing God.
I lied identifying him— we are the
   flesh's fire
not that residue there, not slag!
The dwarf leaked coldness, his face
   fine featured
but squashed, and pure white:
I had stumbled into nightmare.
How had he closed my father's mouth
that no one not me could do at the home?
Are the dead blocks of ice we hammer
   we chisel?

I watch a pretty girl as I write.
I imagine her breasts in my mouth
her milk, the rich cream of life: I need
an image to banish my father's
that rolls into view with his dwarf
when I make love, when I sit in the sun
when I examine my guilts, when I
recall our long rivalry, all unneeded.
I should have lied the truth, "No,
   that's not him":
what would they have done? Rolled in
   a series of stiffs?

'No, not him. Not him, no. Sorry, no'
but as usual I conformed. "Yes," I said,
and the hearse took him off; "Yes,"
and the dwarf wheeled him out.

Later when I walk by the ocean beneath
   the Milky Way
as I have done since I was ten
to find silence and self to frame
the tensions we call living,
I fit words to the surf's rhythms, like
"Live, there is only living, each star
lives in its own milky fire; the hottest
blood burns in the coldest water:
why, father death lives in our flesh
to free us from anxious self-knowledge
when that burden grows too great"—
but I know these only gloss the unpleasant
   truth:
he must fade the way he died, by inches...

There should be more to us when we live.
There should be more to us when we die
than a bleaching like a photo left in the sun—
we aren't mayflies for a season,
not one of the countless ants:
but he after one "I don't know if I can do this"
faded steadily into distance, aware   helpless
   acquiescent.
                    Better to go mad.
Only now, after so many years listening
do I know what the waves really say
as they beat against my anger:
forgive   forget   forgive   forget   forgive

HAUNTING

A wind wheels over the meadow
and breathes through my mind
as I relax by an empty house.
Clear across the bog I see the fox's corner
where the dogs always slaver against
their chokechains. Inside, I hear
a faucet turn, water run, stop, a footstep fall.
I *know* it's my friend's dead daughter, Canda,
wandering where she once lived.
I freeze, changed utterly in a second, afraid
of whatever comes through
when the wall between worlds, tumbles.
The next moment I *know* it's not her
but my father touching unfamiliar things,
a door   a faucet   a drawer
treading a strange hallway, his breath
making a daddy longlegs tremble,
determined to find me and never let go.
I'm terrified... My friend calls, *Lance*—
I breathe, myself again, but what is that—
how easily I walk with the dead,
whether ghostly or just some bodying
of guilt and loss! I worry at that
like a dog at a fox's scent: I imagine
I slip my chokechain and dash
into those shadows folded into the light,
teeth bared, snarling, sure of my prey,
and find myself stumbling among presences
just this side of known... At a loss,
I turn a faucet: water runs through my flesh

like blood. I tread a strange hallway,
make the spider tremble in turn,
touch an arm— *Please, I'm lost, don't run,
don't freeze so in terror at my face—
I only want to go home—* .
I snap to. Now I know what sound
teases just beyond the edge of hearing:
it is the sound walls make when they crumble—
and walls are always falling down.

BY LOVE'S DOING

    Blind in this darkness
I edge over the smallest rise, afraid
        to fall,
the ocean's weight on my shoulders;
or recoil from accordioned wrecks
as I follow the dream thread to caverns
that open and shut like mouths.

    I stop:
my father's body whitens that dark
where death is the only light—
or a window full of sky where I press my
        three year old face
shines before me, full of inexpressible longing
for a father always walking away.

    So I imagine
until the woman beside me flutters the sheets,
        hot-limbed, restless,
so long unable to wake me as I dreamed.
I am painfully sad, and think
I whitened those depths, but slid away
when I tried to touch my own death.

    I'm not sure what images are true:
we always try to give face to the inexpressible,
or discover one story disguises another,
even feel sorrows we only fear may come—
        like I may rehearse in a past loss
the death I will owe at the end.

    Only the pain is sure, and entire.

    I reach for the woman, desperate
to be pulled into flesh, love, life
    by love's doing,
               away
from that marrowed pain, from my childish face
pressed full of longing to the window;
    from knowing now love will leave
whatever I do to make it stay.

VIRGIN SPRING

Is my rage done, plowed into the meadow,
grief let loose in the rain, the desperate drive
   to change everything
burned out by distance and sun, as much to say
time is space   heat   loam   leaf in the air?
How quickly loss doesn't matter, not really, not
after the first boil of blood, whatever trace
   stays in memory:
for what grief goes on intense now as then—
some too intense knowledge there is no
but there for the grace of God go I
   when all go that way;
some balanced likening of self to self lost
so we go on grieving after father death
mother death   child death   for ourselves?
For me life breaks in, fog, rain, sun, the stars
   on clear, crisp nights,
wind, love, those still here or newly come.
We are the blood pumped through the great
   heart of things,
driven in spent and expelled readied
   for new losses—
like leaves that pile on the ground, decay,
   sink down, become rare
lady slippers in the woods or shoots
that crack concrete, delicate yet steady as steel.
Nothing is still, nothing stops.
Even the words that died into my loss
I could not imagine returning, return
when all seemed used, misused, and done,
gushing from my ground in a virgin spring.

LATE SPRING

Where has it hidden, this late spring?
Only now pheasants call like rusty gates
   forced open,
the air at last so warm and clear
Great Point Light is visible over twenty miles
   of Sound.
Heat ribbons the pines' resin through the trees,
and robins, in a fur of feathers in flight
seize the moment to mate and mate and mate.

And I— two years tending my father's dying—
peer into the marsh where ducks talk in tones
   of low strings breaking,
herding their young from shadow to shadow
as fox and coyote hunt the watery verge
and hawks swing between the day moon
   and dry, white sun,
their hunger patient, and penetrative as a
   ray of light.

Two years... Medicines, treatments, hopes
tidal in their lift and fall, and at all times
the slide towards the fire
however we mate or pay to drug ourselves
   with the latest wonder—
why shouldn't age greet death instead as
   Friend,
have you come to end my suffering?

Tomorrow storm will whiten the hollows
   between the groves,

whiten the leaves, whiten the sky, whiten
the air with slashes of cold, pale rain
however my heart hungers for summer
   like a fire under snow.
No wonder I yearn for purpose

as clear as coyote or fox or hawk
who set hunger on foot or give it wing,
but I am left just words for loss, for lateness,
   for the late blooming of relief,
words that matter, sure, and promise an end
but are not flesh not bone but air in my mouth
   absence in my belly,

coals in my brain.

SOFT WEATHERS

I lived my father's long dying
spreadeagled in the bog through a two year
  winter:
sleet-slashed, sleeked by frozen rain
I gleamed in the cold light in primary hues,

all that time unable to move,
grief layered in snowfall on fall,
covered by floodtide for months, still
still except for the slow ooze of mud

embracing my flesh before, finally,
spring's ebbtide bared me, stunned,
  to this sun.
I sit up as the cranberry beds
lift through the ebb,

blink in the light, dazed, unsteady
  when I stand,
and wash in the stream,
cross naked to firmer land
where the oaks are new leaved with suns,

gay streamers hanging from their boughs.
I feel grass in my toes, and smell
its hayscent where mown, taste
the musky pink vulva of lady slippers

inviting me to dim recesses—
I forgot so much, giving my senses to my
  father...

My face opens in this light,
lianas of paradise flowers entwine my arms,

rugosa roses thicket my legs. My tongue
croaks like a crow from a height,
loosens, speaks winds in a whoosh of wings,
speaks— god knows— of the forgetting
  in renewal,

of the loss of what seemed beyond loss
that turns out, in this heat-drugged air
to be something I can't even name:
speaks as though I always spoke

warm light   clear skies   soft weathers...

PEACE

Alpine meadow... A brook spills over stones
to merge far below with the ocean-bound,
gray-green glacial Adige.

Near peaks shake off their covers
and yawn toothily in the sun,
gleaming like new-polished lanceheads.
I burn aware with them, coughing,

sip water coldly pure as a knife in my lungs,
free at last to be ill, in myself, recover, be well,
the duties due the dying, well done...

Each to its own— death, mountain, brook,
a man alive to climb to fall and again work uphill
to the high place where the waters start to gather
the deep peace of the sea.

ESCAPE

Manhattan's summer evenings
steamed rings of dirt around my neck...
We found a beach flung between sea and bay,
a house hung on the dunes,

one nestled later in bayside rushes
that shook their silks in the dark like girls
    when embraced.
Light blazed from sky and sea and land
    and burned me blond,

sand in my hair, my pockets, between
    my toes:
mornings I netted blue claws, hard or soft,
and burrowing fiddlers always freed,
or heel-and-toed for clams, young flounders
    underfoot,

milky light leaning on the bay.
John and Buddy, Guy and Eddie,
Phyllis and freckled Alice,
the girl I loved each summer,

tried to teach and tame me
but I loved nature more, happiest
alone by the ocean at night,
stars, long lunar sands, waves weaving

great distances into me until I learned
to know myself the part of these grown

       self-aware.
That night sea beats in me still—
all comes, all comes, all comes

those waves drum,
words that give and take my peace
now as when despite all I felt alone
and made solitude my friend.

KIDNAPPED

Grizzled as grandfather, my kidnapper's
flesh sagged from age and vice, and I knew
he lied when he stopped me in the street
to say my parents sent him as my guide.
I hated his fetid breath, the adventure

he embodied, yet followed him inside
some tenement, anyway. I clutched
the railing with one hand, my bike
with the other. I was silent. He breathed
into my face and touched my ass, saying

what a good boy I was and did I want
to do wrong and disobey my mother and father?
He grew old and insecure as I stared.
No   I said abruptly.
He understood, and sighed, and let me go.

Why did I follow him? I was amazed
I had a choice and could give that man
what he never thought to force, free
to follow a dark thread in my heart
to a welcomed evil. That is like love—

a sudden presence wholly there,
a song we can't help humming
until freed by an equally blind recoil,
as when I hurried back into the light, dazed
at how easily I could go wrong.

MY BEST FRIEND

Heaven is one block from hell in New York.
My friend found my home all plush—
I found his all linoleum: we sensed
how cold the world is, and unfair.
One Christmas we rode new bikes
along the East River Promenade,

free for a weightless hour of that fate
opening doors for me closed to him:
then he crashed, the frame bent as a body
dropped seven floors. He wept
bearing it home. That summer
polio drove me from his block,

though he was untouched:
when I went to private school that fall
I left his world as surely as though
I had flown to the moon.
Did he rebel when older, go Beat and hate
the world with flowers and love,

yet when the draft notice came,
leave for Vietnam anyway?
We never escape our flaws,
though we learn the universe does not care
who we are or whether we are good
or if that knowledge frees us to live better
  than we do.

What could we say if we met again,

smiled, shook hands, searched for names?
We are old enough to know
the past and time are never equally good,
   or kind;
to prize survival higher, and the warmth
when shared that makes the world less cold.

HARD GRACE

Here is a picture: children gathered
by a halloween bucket, dunking apples...
Even now I feel my mouth agape,
teeth sliding on the shining skin

as laughter and water mix in my throat.
Half choking, I press the apple against
the rim and bite through, smearing juice
and pulp against my palate, eating triumph.
The room is dim as memory's glow,

or the hue of sadness for the family idyll
I and my two mothers tried to uphold
against my father's lies.
Empires rise and fall,

millions die while we go on
modest, private, untouched, with time
for the slow miracle of forgiveness
to grow between my father and myself.
Sometimes great events do not outweigh

small, or measure good and evil,
but let some lives have a second chance
while so many more go down unjustly,
with no chance at all to atone.

ANNIVERSARY CARD

They dazzled rooms they entered,
one dark, one blond, together all
we mean by beauty. My father bragged
of his beauty queen queen of New York
models, this icon to be envied.
But even then he was unfaithful
with some singer, an affair fanned
by his mother who hated mine,
      'that shiksa.'
Phone calls were monitored, letters
steamed open, a detective hired
to undo father's lies— yet after this
I found mother in his lap in glad tears.
Were they each other's forbidden fruit?
Did they love their own beauty,
seeing themselves in each other's eyes?
Or were they just two young lovers love
lifted past their faults for love's season?
When did love stop being enough?
To think, in Venice, she returned
fatigue to ardor, or much later
reduced him to prodding pillows
      and brushes
assembled to mime herself in bed
in the separate room where she slept,
asking:
      My dear, is it you?
to find she had fled with his bankbooks.
Yet for forty years they exchanged
the same anniversary card with

a new year's greeting, a rite continued
even when he remarried. At last
she kept the card, ending even
the *deja vu* love's memory had become
with a final, puzzled shrug.

LIVE IN THE LIE OF LOVE

Again his image haunts me,
my marbled father on his trolley
with his guardian dwarf

who shut his mouth in the cadaver palace.

He shrinks me to impotence,
lashes conscience with the guilt of survival,
and wants me to say

I am the ice sculpture lying there—

that he is my soul's all-too-human image,
my drive to death denied until now.
I won't do it. All winter

I feed the fire of my woman's flesh

to banish this haunting, but as often
sputter and fail as flare. Still, I know
only when I live in the lie of love

can I send death to death once more.

WINTER GARDENS

Lilac blooms along Park Lane,
roses among hips swollen red:
the fragile stems of fuchsia
spangle red droplets among
      the tireless chrysanthemum.
Eight weeks from now bulbs rise
and spring is named regardless:
here winter must come soon or
lose its natural place, although

a season in doubt amazes me—
as if Mars could reverse course
or earth spin towards my youth.
Nature may get small respect
      but nature is all
though being is relative to place
and place is anchored in rules.
In mine I grieve less for my father
than for loss itself.

The shortest day falls now—
I almost said the longest—
there is a place in my heart where
opposites lie side by side, where
      gone is the same as here,
arrive another word for parting:
where the quickest sunset hangs fire
all the years it takes my heart
to let one time go for another.

AGAINST THE GRAIN

November's steady heat teases
    false white blossoms from the plum
and makes narcissus bloom so strongly
    I veer from its reek.
Jasmine flowers a profuse white
    the opposite of snow;
flocks of parrots tear and scream
    as if an endless summer sky
can absorb any damage they do.
    The dream that autumn, that winter
will never come seduces me,
    though my old men are dying
and drag me in their wake into age,
    though this false summer
will be swept away like
    young sweaty ecstasies.
Yet if the mature measure of the real
    cannot be pushed aside forever,
I will dream with my eyes open.
    Let time rain into them.
Let years plump not runnel my cheeks.
    Lie with me... Dream with me...
We choose how we live.

II / Passages

ON THE BEACH AT QUIDNET

All winter my urgent need builds
to return to eastern shores—
others may wander painlessly, pawns
to their trades, but I know peace only
on native ground. I return
when the weather warms
and dive into brisk Atlantic waves.
Blue deepens to green, water streams
down my flesh and flashes
in the light as my arms wheel.
I remember August days
when the sea mirrors the sky,
deep water clear to the bottom,
or in autumn how hurricanes
heap waves into walls whose dare
to climb and ride I once answered
fearlessly. I never dreamed
as I lay on the beach below the stars
that I could age, or be afraid.

I hunt the tideline for some talisman
forged in earth's youth and fire,
white quartz, smoky, or rose...
I will hurt my hands squeezing
those stones in my California exile
to remember how winter stormcaps
whiten the waves, and slant cold rain
gnaws and gouges the cliffs and heaps
sand on long, barren strands,
for the hunger to be whole and

young and home will burn in me,
and it will not help to think of
the great pattern where some things
are lost as others are begun
as I explore the downward turn.

PASSAGES

I am ripe with a season of hunger fulfilled yet
   not relieved,
a river full to the flood mark but still as
   stone, no bitterns poised in hunger
      as in spring;
a millwheel still as windmills' sails on
   windless days.

The old man in his nursing home counts the
   leaves barely singed gold or red outside
      and thinks not yet:
passion breathes on a girl's neck and slides
   its silk down her thighs tingling
      as she thinks not yet;
leaves hold their green as if nothing
   must change.

But when the north wind says *now* in
   crystal tones
the pent waters settle with an audible sigh;
brilliant leaffall lulls the old man to sleep
   past sleep;
the girl wakes in a man's arms flesh melded,
   seed stirring.

I follow the waters to the wide, receding
   shore and flame in the cold as I
      walk home:

You think too much of things that run out
  or play with pain and change or
tangle with one another and grow confused
  my woman tells me.
Oh love, there is no need to gloss
  the beauty everywhere,
only to speak of the fearful damage
  that blinds us to how
ripeness can hurt and loss be beautiful.

THE CHURCH AT OVINGDEAN

Concussive, without memory, workmen
      hammer, drill, saw,
         power lines acoil or
aslither before the altar.
      Full of our old young ache
         for undying love, their
music pounds the Norman nave
      pleinsong,
         matins to vespers,
not even a slow echo
      in the stone. Beyond
         only Ovingdean is saved by law—
Brighton swells to the west
      and the algal creep
         of bungalows oozes
down the eastern shore
      or spreads up the Downs
         to barrow-haunted crests
whose green hides sheathe their ruins.

What can I say, nestled
      in parkland mountains
         in Los Angeles,
while elsewhere the land
      and those before us
         and their works
go down in our willing
      loss of history and resource?
         All we build, so much
more than our fathers,

>   nourishes hard hands
>   violent hearts
> comfort laced with fear.
>
> The hill's lung
>   rises and falls
>   as twilight's gray wave curls
> over and down.
>   Hues laid side by side
>   hint at forms:
> a burst of gulls, a
>   wavering of house and
>   distant city, trees
> become their own shadows,
>   gravestones turning strangely
>   soft. Homing cattle
> low on cue: the throb
>   of rock and roll grows
>   leaden in this air.
> All seems a show staged
>   to laughter or sorrow
>   or hissing we never hear.
> The last bee hunts
>   nectar from the last
>   lit flower in the graveyard—
> finally, silence.
>
> Felt, unheard, a humming
>   fills my ear— nature's
>   great force mutely

singing in the bone
        to tell me I am wrong,
           that these great losses
are furrow and seed
        of the new beauty
           and life to come,
of the new words and
        rhythms for our flesh
           to pray
for the same unchanging love.

HOTEL-DIEU, NOVEMBER

The fields lie fallow... White rows
of stakes mark endless graveyards
that green and burst in season.
Yellow and purple chrysanthemums
stream from high windows, and blackbirds
swarm the fretted steeples as though

five hundred years of tending
the sick and poor have not ended.
But the Sisters who cared have gone—
only tourists like myself come now,
and buyers of the vineyards' pick
who gather here each fall.

My heart is like this place,
fallow and ripe, caring and grown
calculating, so that I recall youth
as these halls history, to find
something better than this present
coldly mature air. Yet sometimes

when warmth wells up from depths
where hardy blackbirds never fail to sing,
I cease to envy those loved poor, and feel,
surprised, a grace like one of their
vanished Sisters move through me,
ministering solace hurt by hurt.

Beaune, Burgundy

THE DEATH OF A SPARROW

Once I slung a stone in my new slingshot
and slew a sparrow. But when I looked
into his still living eye, full of knowing,
that look carved into bone.
Did I end his misery or just walk away—
even now remorse blinds memory.
Should a small death matter so?

A sparrow's death mirror the world's fate
where men rush to kill
habit-hardened, hateful, remorseless?

Is evil absolute in each act, threaded
into the texture of the day? Or relative,
tolerable-to-past-forgiveness? To whom?
Does God know? Does God care?
Does our blood's steam vanish into air
without meaning? Where is an ark
whose tablets settle these questions?

I walked away unwilling to kill again
without thought... When I crush
swat   smash   or cook   eat

what was alive I do only what I must.
How heavy my feet felt as I left that sparrow...
Every part of my body felt aware.
His death threw me into care.
Fifty years later I still see him there—
his eye full of fear stares at me
from the marrow of my heart.

PLAYS WITHIN PLAYS

Strange, this sky— a fin of fire cruises westward:
  naptha beams— flame throwers in an
    otherworldly war—
boil the clouds and choke the light:
  Vs of geese, and lower, a cloud of crows
    fly swiftly through the murk.
Another moment, and the sky transforms
  to gold tissues, some lamé, and darkens
    by stages to navy, glittering strands
as though a dancer shedding veils.
  A last orange flutter of coals,
    and night draws a curtain over the field.
Who is watching? I wonder, chilled
  suddenly sure all this is a show
    for an audience behind the sky
for whom even now I am part of the play,
  the hero in the dark.
    Who sees me for what I am?
Am I anyone at all?
  Or am I married to a role called 'myself'
    that turns out instead to be all mask?
I scurry from the field,
  confused by the doubts
    the black hawk of anxiety
lives to slide down the wind and strike.
  I hesitate at my door:
    love, and light, are there, and those
who will give me a name and place, pleased
  I am home,
    wondering what kept me—

how can I share my fears
   and make their happiness insecure?
    I go in quietly,
answering smile with smile.

BUDDHA IN LOS ANGELES

Where is there peace? where death
as black beaks tear ripe persimmons
above a fallen glory of orange leaves?
Already narcissus blooms and violets
purple green shadows in this hot now
cold now summer now winter air.
I feel surreal as images jumbled on film,
unsure who I am, or when. I burst
in white flames from the tips of irises,
sink mineral by mineral to bulbs
with greedy lips, and nourish a secret root
as rain falls aromatic and sweet
from high eucalyptus leaves where
fog's cold streamlets tangle and grow thick.
I'm wrong wanting to island myself
from this flood— even silence fills with
my blood singing, while sleep becomes
another waking. And though my heart
calls anything but its own eternity *the end*,
death only changes one life to another,
here. No one can escape. All I can do is
     live deeper.

DREAMS

Some dreams strand me in tenements
where light is the color and density
of solid dust. They tower overhead and
plunge into the abyss beneath my feet,
stuffed with frozen lives as I

thread my way in fear and loathing
to a single lit room I never reach
in the bowels of a building. Sadness
pierces my ribs and squeezes
my heart. Each time I learn

I am forsaken.

I choose to live in Wyoming's
lunar wastes, and below the Dakotas'
continental skies, and where the Pacific
gnaws its boundaries, enormous,
slothlike, sure to succeed.

Such large spaces drive me in, erase
and release me. They make large sins
seem small. Because it has nothing,
because in these places everything
has yet to come, my heart fills

again, for a time, with innocence.

WHY JEFFERS STILL BUILDS TOR TOWER

an elegy after Robinson Jeffers

Five years Jeffers wrestles stones uphill
      to Hawk Tower
in brilliant light or gray, burned or soaked and
chilled by the heavy-shouldered heave of winter
surf roaring on the granite shore
   he quarries.
Muscles clench and loosen, grow hard as
   quartz, fluid as wave:
                      when he pauses,
he stares into storm and finds God in its
   heart, still
building this world as he his tower.

Done, he prowls the tower's rampart,
driven to poems heavy with granite's old fire,
and the waves' long heave, winter light, and
   chance warmth,
each enough for itself, like men are in God's eyes,
one called forth for his good, another for his wrong
as surely as day alternates with night
however we call ourselves free.

Years pass like ships on the horizon.
He loses love and, bitter, wrestles death to a draw
in hard supple songs that make his conflicts
   our own—

even now from Hawk Tower in kelp-
   sharpened air as
a seal coughs rounding the point in calm,
   summer waves,
and light swells out of the west that here
   turns east, infusing all
with a crimson glow that unstrings the will,
he labors on his ramp, back arched as a
   drawn bow, muscles working like
water over a reef as he rolls his life uphill,

for no tower, however high hands dipped in
   sweat and granite and song may build
can bind the restless and unmoving
or reach that place where peace abides,
   and be done.

HARRY'S PLACE
AT HAMPTON COURT PALACE

Catherine screams in the raven gloom
whom Harry loved, and every Tudor Tom and...
She was a true Tudor rose who knew one
   season only:
ever-opening.

Harry cut off her head.

Greater Wolsey sighs where recent fire
bared his stuffy gilded study,
throat so dry sandpaper in the sun is damper.

He lost everything to Harry over another skirt—

only death cheated Harry of his doom.
Why do they stay when they could ride belief
clear of our flesh instead of watching me, now,
with no soul to lament

walk through their old rooms in January?

Imagine how Catherine felt before condemned,
a pure fragrance in impassioned air
touching every hand, held by none:

or Wolsey, more surely feared

in the company of his peers than the tomb:
and how his throat muscles strangled him

at the end, and Catherine
woke to reality when the crowd roared

as falling steel sliced her neck:

what surprise
what bitterness to discover
they weren't immune from our plain state.

Who would not have stayed reproaching
   Harry? Brutal

conscience-clear, faithless rhyming Harry
who led them through these gardens,
savoring the freshly severed head of the
winter sun swelling on the horizon.

ABERFOYLE

Sun... Rain... Hail... Snow
   on Ben Lomond, rainbows—
this could have been my home
   in beauty. Who would not
have fought to keep this theirs—
   and been driven across the sea
to the Alleghenies by steel after
   the last charge at Culloden,
or by loss, or desire, or a need
   for a lesser sky, a kinder air.
Like a blind man given sight
   violence would have torn the veil
of belonging to the world,
   and they would have seen their
strangeness and known their exile
   was the common condition. We are
never able to deny the losses in time
   that time, for time, makes us pay.
Now the stiff wind topples
   shallow-rooted Norwegian pines:
loosened earth silts the loch—
   Ard—Voil—Venachar— ...
Charcoal heaps mark old forges
   that hammered plowshares into swords:
no cries from children, calls by men,
   penned cattle, morose bulls, their horns
and long fur quaking from desire
   break this stillness:

no oak or peat smoke mars my view
   from the terrace, tea sipped,
eye on beauty the mind draws
   with a half-guessed half-baked romance
over the lessons of the past.

HANNIBAL / AT SIXTY

First mites attacked, all those hovels
between royal guestrooms whose faded gilt
Roman threats expelled me from—
    killing them
takes forever. Next a tooth chipped,
Expensive, unseen, an Egyptian sighed,
his fingers under my tongue
    Let it go:
at your age all recoveries are partial,
the lost parts of the body become
omens of the soul's fate. That winter
    a cold brought
gum ulcers: a Babylonian in a slum
did nothing, too— they left
reluctant as lovers to part.
    My knees buckled
next— *You're worn,* a Greek Hippocrates
said: *something in your knee has torn,*
you'll heal, but always have a gimp.
    I thought of battles
I survived hardly scathed, no wound
worse than a hook in my thumb
instead of a fish when nine—
    or was I ten?
How far behind is death, eager
to plant us in time and place,
when we lose the dates of our pain?
    Better to have died
at Zama, the Roman death machine
all swords all javelins all my long lines

bared by my own cavalry:
    to have died the
Martyred Hero of a lost Cause,
not gone from thick king to king
urging they fight before the Romans
    picked the gold
from their heads and teeth. Now
I let them find me by this shepherd's hut.
The archers circle—
    they come no closer—
they still fear me, when the future
is what tears all that matters from a man.
Their arrows nock and release—
    find me oh Death
a feathered heap in tufts of sheep wool
and dusty, beetle-riven dung,
bald, old, absurd, spared.

CRONE

She chews soul-rinds, rheumy eyes
    cataract white, pushing her cart
full of what age   illness   mischance
    leave of our tragedies and joys.
Her sweater is torn, worn pink
    grown gray, a find to replace a tunic,
as that a toga, the toga deerskins
    hugged close to replace the fur
that once sheathed us as we swung
    limb to limb. She was always
wood brittle, steel tough.
    She knows less of who she is
or what she does than a stone.
    Abruptly, I see through her— no
black robes, hood, death's head,
    skeleton or scythe: no:
her creamy skin glows,
    her black hair shines blue—
but the same fixed smile sits
    on red, ripe lips, and her eyes
though bright are just as vacant.
    She is a force without freedom,
a kiss without love, love
    without heart, a careless beauty
who can never be ours or even her own.
    At the end my sheets will become
the shroud-sails my last breath
    will puff into her arms:
she will take me as though
    a scrap from the street... For now

let her wheels grind into distance.
      I hold my life firmly, although
even stone seen in the right light
      billows and eddies and flows.

ACTAEON

> *Great was the chase with the hounds for the*
> *unattainable meaning of the world.*
> *. . . Czeslaw Milosz, "Winter"*

Actaeon's fingers are spring leaves
   in a light breeze on lyre-strings, the
     outward echo of how a surgeon touches
the heart's web of arteries and veins.
   The lord and lady, warriors, dogs, servants,
     the roar of flames in the hall still
as he noses a spoor of song to the story's lair
   where a man half animal waits,
     or heroes clash sword to shield,
or a woman and her lover thrash
   where her angry mate enmeshes them.
     None stir: what loss   triumph   shame
defines a life that echoes their own?

He leaves them late,
   the flare of truth replaced
     by twined flesh and lovecries.
Black streets, a simple room, old maidservant,
   bread and water, payment tossed aside—
     he wants another gold.
His pupils come at first light, slight boys
   to teens whose shoulders thicken
     who chafe to be men, lethal and heroic,
bulls with girls.
   But Actaeon leads them like wild horses
     around and around a corral

with a rope of fables.
   This world he says *is a story*
     waiting to have its meaning laid bare.
Listen— and listen: look, and look until
   the breeze becomes words, the shudder
     of leaves, flesh, the river murmur,
dialogue, stone a Yea! or Nay!

They leave aroused, the commonplace
   given a mysterious sheen.
     On impulse he calls his old hound,
back bent like a bow,
   and walks under the noon blaze
     the same white as the streets
where so many hide behind their walls, wise
   to avoid being caught in some moment
     life writes in red,
to be instead the audience stories feed.

He reaches the forest where even shade is hot.
   The hound laps water from the stream
     like a machine.
Actaeon edges along the bank as though
   tracking some scent to its source.
     When the waters grow wide and calm
a small stream courses off.
   Something as light as spring leaves
     in a light breeze
touches his neck and makes his hair rise:
   he whirls— no one— someone—

     something
he senses that does not act
   but watches without pity or cruelty,
     amused, sad, will-less.
The hound's hair ridges down his back.
                                     Come
   he commands, choosing the unknown way.
     The beast follows,
back straightened, a snarl gleaming in his eyes.

Actaeon finds himself hurrying until
   branch-whipped, thorn-torn,
     his breath a curlew's whistle,
his heart a roar of waves, he falls
   against the hard *No* of the earth
     and jams moss muskily into his mouth.
When he looks up, the grotto.
   A small rivulet arches over a cliff, the
     movement of sun on water spring leaves
in a light breeze.

   She is there,
     flesh flawless.

He gapes, and stands carelessly, staring.

   Their eyes meet *and he understands*

   She is a young girl on her bridal bed,
the shy husband,

    their tremble, penetration, joy:
        and She is a sword raised high,
its perfect edge,
    a stream of blood blurring its sheen,
        a head rolling on the ground;
boys who give grace its meaning
    as they arch and ache
        against one another in the gymnasium;
the smoke of incense, of crematoria,
    bitter flesh driven unwilling to the fire,
        the fire;
the choking dust across the battlefield,
    the blind men, thrusts, wounds,
        the flowers around their graves,
the spring leaves, the light breeze;
    the newborn's howl,
        its mother's smile,
the birth blood wiped from a new face;
    the whitecaps on the sea, the sea,
        the wave that swallows men in their boats,
the swallowed men,
    the fish that gnaw them bone white,
        the bones:
and the grieving heart that begins again,
    that risks love to find love—
        and love's betrayal.
She lets all wounds be forgotten
    and tirelessly gnaws the heart's red bone,
        bringing all to perfection,
kind or cruel, Her beauty

   the only mold,
      the truth at the end and beginning
of every story.

Actaeon does not reflect
  A man must do what he can,
     and beyond that be content
—no, he has found what he wants
  and screams, and runs

     runs as though horns grow from his head
and an animal bellow pours from his throat,
   as though hounds leap to the chase,
     as though he is the hounds and the hunted,
the teeth, the torn flesh,
  the terror, bright blood
     and the final heartful, heart-rending
horror, and delight.

EURYDICE

My blood sings to his words
   because they give me myself;
I love his hair tousled over his brow
   or combed back, bouffant: love
how he flings his clothes on or off,
   his belly a touch too rounded,
his cheeks smooth or unshaven,
   his long-fingered hands on me
deer in a forest, sometimes certain,
   sometimes all flight. I love even
his worn unwashed machismo:
   I am all flowing scales and sudden,
plucked ecstasies. Why, today
   he made silence sing, dancing
before a great heron—
   the wary bird was entranced
by his body's music, and I,
   and the sea, who stilled her waves.

But he lives only for crests—
   when I want to wash clothes,
comb hair, shave cheeks,
   listen to another's song grow in me
he goes mad— *Me me me* sounds
   behind every word,
each restless shift of arm and leg:
   he turns from rain on dry land
to rain on floods, snow
   on snowdrifts, sleet on ice.
I become his levee, plow, salt,

anything to contain, order, melt:
it doesn't matter what face mirrors mine—
   I am because I change.
Slowly as he before the heron
   I learn a new word, and leave.

He turns to animals who love purely—
   birds who perch on his shoulders,
snakes uncoiling from the hollow
   of his emptiness, dogs
panting under hand, lions
   who sleep with lambs.
He craves God in a crystal, love
   in a string tuned high 'C,' all
but moaning *I can't get no*
   can't get no   no satisfaction though
he never sings another's lyrics.
   There is always pain enough,
why add more? I think, and return.
   You are in hell I say, giving words
to him now: *follow me— I will lead*
   you out if you obey...
He fawns at my heels...
   We seem in a tunnel
with light ahead, or in the light
   with darkness swelling...
My genius, he murmurs, *transforms.*
   I start to believe this time
this time   this time   but I see
   he thinks only 'humor the woman,

lead by seeming to obey.'
  I stare him from sight.

Later, he lies— I hear
  in that hell we share
from fear sharing is a dream
  and we are locked in ourselves,
that love is the illusion
  which lets us bear our loneliness.
Perhaps it doesn't matter —
  someone always wants more
than he can have, someone's heart
  is broken, another's, mended,
someone stays in hell,
  another moves on.

I am surrounded by children
  and presumptions I humor
from the one true virtue, kindness.
  The music here is sparse
yet beautiful because all there is:
  I no longer live in the poverty
of its hope to be more.

REMBRANDT TALKS ABOUT HIS WOMEN TO ME

"What stick arms jut beside swollen breasts
   that sag on flabby mounds
while thighs flood wide as smaller women.
   I saw how far we can fall from grace,
until only fit to be rolled naked
   down a dirty street.
Even my wife swells under her robes,
   but red-lipped, swollen cheeked and
candy fleshed, breasts heaped and stomach
   ready to be bared, pressed, licked,
squeezed, sucked in measure to how much
   I wanted to eat beauty.
                            Forget the portraits—
they paid to be seen like that
   though even those lack your worship
of thinness even when it maims.
   Maybe I was careless to measure women
by warring waves of hate
   or lust for life unending—
I was full of myself, godlike, young.
   But look at you in your Cafe—
a woman hacks beside you,
   smoke burns your eyes and grays the air
like a low fog over a field
   and music throbs in your temples
as you flip through my gallery of extremes,
   straining to understand,
your soul wracked with hunger.
   Yet you were careless of beauty too

until your wife grew a scar back to breast
   and wrote "we die" in your heart: until
a daughter cut from steel lay unconscious,
   her brain swelling like forgotten fruit
in a cupboard, while you ate and ate
   to bury death under ham haunch arms
and thighs—with that madness
   you must understand mine!
Later, my wife dead young, son frail,
   few commissions, passed by by style,
bankrupted, disrupted, desire
   a girl's clothes torn by a maddened mob,
I saw life is little and easily harmed as flesh,
   though that is tougher than the soul it sheathes,
the hidden fire any draft blows out.
   I dissolved my silks and brocades
into rough brush strokes, knife smears,
   finger moldings over the bareness
nothing clothes long,
   and married desire's dream to disease
that martyrs even the corrupt,
   and to water's tremble because
someone I loved made it tremble, because
   love trembles from knowledge of its end.
Where I lie is cold as a rasp on ice.
   Your Cafe is sickroom stuffy.
Day disappears into its rags and blankets.
   The waitress hurries as if 'to be' is 'to rush,'
and it is. And now?
                    Say with me:

'I am done denying the truth is plain,
a lit window to walk towards
   where someone I love waits for me
to grow old with her if only
   I will come in from the false dream
there is anything about us to waste.
   I am become water, and tremble
from my love's least touch.
   I am become the hurt of desire
that deepens with time and makes
   simple things the most precious to hold.'"

EROS IN PICCADILLY

I ride some rare beautiful sound
    that should change the world
unaware until I reach the landing.
    Almost I go down to tell her and leave
some large gesture in her case,
    but I will myself smaller and go out
where Eros is garish above crowds
    I blur into, moneyed and avid.
I feel plain as pavement, betrayed,
    that I am to blame, even if
turning from beauty is an old thing:
    I feel I always let myself down, afraid
to answer the call I hunger for
    but ignore and turn on or destroy
if made too strongly.
    Mist falls   rain   sleet   snow.
His glitter goes, and his shape
    while her voice still vibrates in my bones.
Soon just a dim glow remains
    like a beacon winking at sea
amid the rise and fall of waves,
    a homely window that beckons in the dark;
a warning of shipwreck   despair   death;
    the last light in drowning minds
who cling to its beauty
    that changes everyone who answers its call.

III / Through Nature

THIN...

Nothing is visible but
stars chisled from ice
and the slow meteors of planes
above shadowed trees and homes
   down my unlit street.
An owl calls more deeply
than any I've ever heard,
swallowing me whole so now
my eyes see the chisels
   that shape the stars,
and beyond them
the first sky of fire
still embracing the night
that holds me in turn.
   How eagerly I call
for blood like whiskey
in my maw, call
for the tickle of fur
in my gut, careless
   of what life
I take for my own.
Shocked, I sink into myself
aware again of the civil hungers
in these near homes.
   How easy
to shed the thin skin
of humanity, I think,
sleepless after I turn in,
hearing that low call
   in my dark places
where even dreams fear to go.

TRACKS

Here is a hollow sheltered from the raw
   Atlantic wind
filled with gull tracks, web-footed and wide,
taloned wedges of hungry crows,
traceries of sparrows or larks fine as lace,
with one frayed thread wandering off alone...

A silence with wind,
with light spatterings of sand,
with sunlight in full flood
the thud of great waves from the beach—
a symphony then, without man, fills my ears

and somehow, renews.
I imagine a fox, or coyote, or raven
musing over my tracks with these, later,
noting how I paused, then moved on,
wondering what purpose drove me:

when only this silence responds
they blink, trot off, or leap into the air.
I feel a common thread
bind flesh and fang and feather,
these brief moments that let us feel
   our earnest lives

are fresh and sweet as the water
that rises sometimes through a well-pipe
driven into these dunes
however steep the salt sea grows

or fierce the hungers that drive us through

our daily search for deliverance.

IDYLL

Green herons flush at my steps
and drag orange feet through the air
as sprays of sunlight fall through newly
lush trees on damp ground.
Horsetail tufts of wiry grass

waver in the bare breeze
where finely filigreed seeds,
white as dreams, coast the currents.
Here a reader in a pondside arbor,

whose dog frightens minnows in
the shallows, there, heron still,
a lone fisherman, the long beak
of his rod mirrored in still water.
A kingfisher needles to and fro

a white trunk among the green,
stitching deaths together all one
afternoon, while perch drift upward
towards the baited light, and,

deeper, bass, or something longer
and lethal, follow the schools
toward shore. How easily my eye
is deceived, how eager to lie—
to see all this as an idyll...

Pensive, the herons watch from
hidden limbs as we retrace our ways,
leaving silent wakes in the woods,
as though hunters, intent on prey...

STONEHENGE IN WINTER

These stones are never lonely in winter,
nested in grass always green:
even now brown fields are plowed and seeded,
furrows blackened with feasting crows.

Why, the gardens along the roads from town
are full of winter cabbage and chard—
heads of lettuce burst from the ground
and fill the air with green balloons.

These bluestones and grays
are battered seeds left from a larger time
when the land was still unwon, the soil
not fueled by falling generations

now so fused with earth and mind
the engendering root defies all cold,
and fans its veins as deeply in our hearts. Love,
let us make through this demi-winter's afternoon

what the land makes in its hidden fever,
and when we tire, rest in each other
like these stones on the earth's green breast,
whose milk is forever spilling over.

WINTER SOLSTICE

The sunshortened days grow dark
and the wheel of setting rays rolls
weakly on though brash stars glow.

Frenzies of ravens gouge the last
orange persimmons: radiant, the fruit
quivers on skeletal limbs while torn
droppings fall among a sea of violets:
deeper, bulbs already wound the earth.

I tire of denying hope to avoid hurt
when dry winds burn the late-fallen
plum leaves brown and purple the hills,

when redolent narcissus blooms,
dizzying as death and renewal
who war in the blood's red streets.
Now fires leap the ridges and rid
the land of last year's growth

I hunger to burn clean, to feel
a long cold night break the husk
that holds my heart's new green.

A PANTHER IN AN OLD WOOD

A ripe moon touches the green panther
   of the remnant wood
so tightly hemmed against the fence
   his chest takes its imprint:

only his eyes' green glare taste freedom.
   He peers towards the window—
inside the man and woman lie after love
   and hope for a breeze

while his seed ripens deep within her.
   The man dreams himself inside the green glare
caged in the wood, and imagines
   undoing in one green bound

a lifetime of making the land tame
   as the woman by his side.
He wakes suddenly. He feels how his fields
   have worn him down

to make him pay for their fruitfulness,
   and decides to run.
But when she stirs beside him,
   her love cools his heart—

he feels her complete, immediate trust
   cage the beast in his blood.
He plows and plows and plows at dawn
   but not the wood,

however she urges it must go.

THE OWL

Night voyeur, he trails white
afterimages across the yard
and settles on the lopped
white trunk of the sycamore,
head swiveling, the yellow
lighthouse flash of his eyes
searching the night. Near me
a woman sleeps, tired from
flight, from home-coming,
from love-making, passion's
sweet oil on her skin...
The owl stares in the window—

> *he sees her, and*
> *sees nothing: she*
> *is peace and he*
> *hunger, desire,*
> *blood listening*
> *for a heart to*
> *betray itself and*
> *whisper:* come...

I pace our quiet rooms, shining
from the same sweet oil,
listening to his adamant calls,
sure a moment of betrayal
will bare me— not our unguarded
self-betrayals in the shadows,
but the heart's willing slide
toward that victimhood

we are always poised on
because no one can do more
than borrow love for a time
before the loan is called in.

>   Forgive, forget
>   *are not words*
>   *he knows—*
>   *the future is*
>   *a blind man*
>   *he feeds with*
>   *self-knowledge*
>   *just before the end.*

I could feed on our failings too,
yet I forbear in blind deference
to the dire, hard-pressed dare
of the woman's womb to care,
to educate that bloody child,
violence,
to hope and meaning and love.
How his soft calls thrill my blood...
My eyes flash through the night,
and it is very hard to let
any innocence around
go free, and grow, and flower.

COYOTE

New worlds open to me,
steep stone hives that scratch
the night sky littered with light
like dank alleys with drunks
   and food;
and suburban lawns
where children play,
staring at me, amazed—
for I have run the gauntlet
of gun and trap, felt poison
eat through my gut, the earth
reach overhead and the womb
spill me out reborn before
I had time to forget or despair.
I go where I choose—
only shores I never saw before
stop me, waves breaking so unlike
those Pacific waters I knew.
Evenings I gather with my kin
and yip and yowl on
the metal reeds of our throats
such spirals of sound my fur
ridges down my own spine.
Then she comes, crying with
the crying I must sate,
my back arched into a bow,
head arrowed over the ground,
slavering, pent with the promise
to fulfill— and I do— ah, love,
   I do.

Then, at last, peace. And
just past the edge of sound—
in the darkness— darkness itself
singing my song, singing
survival, passage, passion,
  triumph.

THE DOLPHIN

Two a.m. and not even my woman's heat
soothes my guilts or helps me forget
   my father died in terror of being alone
no matter how I wrestled death two years

to soften his decline:
mouth open amazed or in denial
the boat carried him across the river, stripped
   of all that mattered, anyway.

The wind in the junipers echoes the waves'
crash and roll that makes the bedroom tremble:
sheets of spray, shoals and reefs of waverush
and loose sand flood the beach, while the moon

   is braised bright silver to remove its tarnish.
Slowly the only rhythm deeper than a woman's
heartbeat carries me to sleep.
At dawn I walk the throbbing shoreline.

Clouds step on each other's heels
   dark light light dark the way pained scenes
replay themselves, refusing to fade.
Yet I feel like a new man as I race these

down the beach, arms akimbo, while a
dolphin arches through a cresting wave
   and writes on the sea's green curl
Forget, though you are in the sun's crosshairs now,

and death is etched in the heart,
and forgetting is never done—
nature is not something to solve, but live.
   I lift my voice and sing.

MUSKRAT

The sun's eye moves across the still pond
with the island in its center where
muskrat anchors his home.

Does he raise his eyes at night
from his den's lip to stars
arched as if a child's dip and blow
    of soapy bubbles?

Does he see them gleam lilies on the pond
whose stems spear into darkness
like the stars' into the night sky

whose dark weight we only guess?
Does he too live in opposites, love
hate   life   death   now   forever?

All that ever was or could be   is
dust in a box
that needs just one drop of desire

to repeat itself again,
and that one drop falls without stop.
Once he rippled water homewards

with a leafy twig in his mouth—
how many of his kind have fed
generations of summers

and yet always remained the same?

Now winter stills the water.
Somewhere within the island he sleeps,

a mound of graybrown dust in a box.

Contraseasons

> Autumn
> Spring
> Summer
> Winter

AUTUMN

A greater surf pounds the beach— dawns
   grow cold, and evenings:
one morning a last crescent of day moon
   hangs north of the sun,
      and the season falls tartly on the tongue.
Austerities of bright space flood the East;
   metallic sunsets burn the West—
one noon the sea wears the thin, brief glitter
   of a mayfly's wing,
the air silent as those brilliant daubs of color
   that buzzed and clicked and lately fiddled
vanish into the ground...

Cranberries sheet flooded bogs red, then oak
   and maple steal their hues and smolder
      among the pines,
to catch fire like matches in a row under
   skies defining emptiness. Storm clouds
tangle in the trees, snuffing their fire, or
   whirl upward in steaming flames:
when the gray clears, limbs startled bare
scratch winter from the sky, while wind
sweeps away the bright mosaics a
   careless artist laid on the roads
with the deep theme of time's passage, and
   how that passage is beautiful.

The last ducks and geese quawk and honk as
   they lift and leave when
the great wave that rolls up the beach and

    punches through the dunes to resalt
        the moors
hustles autumn into winter, resounding.
We grow afraid of death, white as the winter sky
    at noon, as the breath that runs before us,
        as the ice that held this land in its fist;
of being where all that is, is stark and bare as
    bone nearly stone,
of being old, of wanting without will, and
    knowing ourselves so.

All these draw me from the city of burning
    suns beside the numb Pacific
to stand on native ground and recall
    in lymph and marrow
what gives our hearts the power to go on—
a reality learned first, and deepest, of
    even light, of neither dead cold nor
        thoughtless warmth,
of words that soothe, arms that reassure, and
    the smile that gives winter its lie
        at the doorway to the world.

SPRING

A cold wind blows waxwings through
   calligraphies of winter brush: they are
      old autumn leaves, dun and sear,
with flashes of memory's brilliant reds
   on their wings.
A season's arrested growth of beard stubbles
   underfoot, thin skins
      of ice brittle as old men's
         skein over the pools—
yet there a robin stalks a pond's frozen lip,
   on fire.

Geese pause on the river, splash upwards
   and V north over trees
      where starlings cluster, impatient as
         ill men to be well,
as all men who hunger to be free of the
      cold distance of discomfort
         their drudgery exiles them to:
they ignore the small woodpeckers carrying
      coals on their heads,
like a man anxiety some sleepless 4 a.m.

All is mixed in all, on edge,
      polar wastes and ruined leftovers
         with intimations of new lives:
even the coldest wind burns,
      and no chill is deeper than on
         a summer's day
            or the thought of loss while in

        a woman's arms.
We wait to be young again, patient
            as a clenched jaw
as buds burn yellow and red prints on the
                winter sky
    and green flames twist through the ice,
not wise, not choosing all, but enduring,
as though punished for some sin past recall.

We shudder, and the ground, whose great
    brown wings beat through scribbled stars—
only yesterday they carried us from the light,
            but now
        because they must
      because forgiveness, too, is in
    the nature of things,
they bring us closer and closer to the flame.

SUMMER

Summer is the post-coital movement
   of surfeit that leaves a taste of ashes
      on the tongue—
when behind the blaze of days
   the sun almost forgets to dim
      the year starts to decline
and all moves towards a ripeness
   we must devour to relieve—
      corn that ripens within its silks,
the fattening thighs of roots in the earth,
   melons full-breasted on their vines,
      tomatoes who burst their skins,
then drip on their leaves:

when newmown hay rots in the sun,
   the sweet stench half pleasing,
      like low tidal flats under the
midday broil, or red dulse abandoned on
   the high tide line; when heat
      lifts acrid whiffs of ocean
from dune sand and grass, the sand
   pillowy underfoot that in winter was
      bare and firm, the grass matted
that was thin: when bees fly drunk
   from nectar turned hard in its sac,
      and insects whine and buzz and click
dry cantatas in humid air
   to celebrate another day's survival
      after morning swallows mob their
dazed struggle to rise on damp, sheer

wings. Night grows out of the ground
   in slow, black flowers that open together:
      clouds thicken, secretive as fertile women;
large soft drops slide from the leaves,
   bemused and wobbling.
      This is the season Adam fell, and Eve,
that seems it cannot end,
   when bad air in the cities
      badly mimics marsh miasma and decay,
and sweat and ripening, racking lust
   become a brilliant nightmare—
      when tears sweeten sorrow with their salt
and we wander in a daze from feast to feast,
   gunshot breaks of boughs
      bent by fruit grown profuse
disturbing the night:
   when our hearts hear the year say
   I am the body of eternity —
come, eat...

So summer dominates us all,
   reductive, tyrannical, in velvet boots,
      refusing all offers to surrender,
promoting the party line until the end.
   One day, we wake like a man
      in a field a storm he slept through
has laid waste—
   the air is cold, the sky sanded bare, and
      and we remember
how ardently we deceived ourselves

   thinking *If if only, if*
      we said to a perfect day, *stay*
it would...

Orion climbs into the night,
   a club in one hand,
     running his hounds past harvest past
stubble into the season
   when the heart becomes a stag
     leaping towards colder days.
We remember our dreams with regret
   and hunger to be lean, to relearn
     the meaning of completion
through the hunger at our heels...
   It is this wanting too much,
     this wanting built into our hearts
that brings the lightning down
   that sets our sere flesh aflame,
     like a field we must fire
to nourish another year with ashes.

WINTER

Now death slips into thought and dream
as easily as slumber in my too warm room,
for spring and summer have run
from the shattered jails of the woods,
and my fear all could be stripped
    has come true.

Deer dun as bark or black as shadows
    on new-fallen snow
quiver and stare as silence gathers and ice
matches the lakes' eyes to the sky's white,
while the heart shivers in its cage of bones
exposed as the cardinal in naked woods.

>   *Go down and become nothing,*
>   *feel hope fail, let go the fever*
>   *that fuels the mind with want; go*
>   *into the dark with acid on your tongue,*
>   *grief past tears or words, past even*
>   *the repair of the womb,*
>   *and feel the emptiness of all efforts*
>   *to save those you love.*
>   *Say* All you have done, all
>   known, all thought to store
>   against loss, is futile—
>   *and let that go too, tasting the*
>   *last bitterness of forgetting.*

But what of the heart's and the veins'
    living lava cased

in cold silver finning iced-over depths?
Of life pending in sac and egg or
wrapped in winter silks on winter limbs
though the countless shining wings that
    fed the day

or the crawling things that filled the shadows
    with dread, are gone?
The pond's ice pens spring's thunder in
    its hold, crackling
like lightning as it tightens its grasp,
booming some nights under alert stars
that have rubbed summer's sleep
    from their eyes.

Blue spruce and green fir flare
over summer's smother; ice that sheathes
    the woods all one night
sprays beauty from countless prisms
    in the morning:
by evening snow flashes into being
like fireflies who brighten June evenings,

each flake unique as each of the dreams
that flock together in our minds
    for warmth... In cities
calligraphies of new plays envine marquees
while paintings leaf from gallery walls
and things and things and more
    pile up in windows where passersby

and children press as though these were
corn and wheat and round harvest
	ripenesses.
All want to say *Death has no being* –
though nature is not here or there but where
we stand: what flesh can lose, it will,
	and so spirit, too.

What then does the world mean,
	speaking *winter?* That question
rowels our hearts with its spurs
and the answer we guess even more
whether days are long or nights longer—
the word winter speaks is *love,*

one that contains all of desire and fear,
where we rank no higher than dust
that one day will be part of something
	that lives—one warm morning
penned thunder breaks free from the ice,
and depths that were gray gleam blue

as a clear high noon: what was frozen
in rigor mortis grows supple as pure
energy fuses up from the root where
we sank to find what would be left of
ourselves stripped to the core, now happy

as the first man when the world was new.

GIVEN WING

Black-headed Brants rain from the sky
with white ear feathers on their necks,
turning these tidal flats solid goose.
Waves of them bob in the Bay, or blow

in black ribbons crest to crest:
Vs wing overhead, singing towards
Nantucket and Florida and farther cays,
while westward heavy mists and clouds stifle

the few pale oranges burning the gray.
How wild they are, how little to do with me,
sweeping away summer's dream of a
    moment so full
it need never change. They make me hungry

to break my gold, domestic chain,
to slide singing down the air's cold curve
as feathered, as steady, all will and wind,
the world made visible, and given wing.

DREAMS ARE

Hope lasts years of drought
    until one November's rains
wash away the dust that made
    the land's face a mask.

Cracked lips and cheeks' wrinkles
    fill as though dried fruits reripened:
the tongue's clapper supples
    in the mouth's well.

How long was I sandpaper?
    Pain wipes out time when here
and time erases pain completely.
    Now I dance under the persimmon,

rain sleeking my face, redgold leaves
    slipping from my shoulders
as I slide on the wet grass,
    denying I was ever dry.

Later the last persimmon
    smolders on a bare branch,
the wood dampdark as my tongue,
    every wet leaf glowing,

the air an elixir as steam lifts
    from the soaked ground
in light clear as Eden's.
    All is possible, I think

carried away: death has an end.
    I will always bend but be
too young to break.
    Then hot winds blow

week after week:
    my tongue's clapper
slats against my mouth's wooden bell:
    quick small feet

pick over my runneled ground.
    When wasn't I dry?
Too dry to dream?
    When did dreams not lie?

HERON, CARMEL

A great blue heron watches a man
      dance the slow aggression of tai chi,
all control and fluid interplay.
      Heron   breeze   waves   grow still...
Somewhere tracers brighten the dark:
      a woman weeps; a child topples
one-legged, unable to cry
      from landmine's pain, but here
man and heron are the stillness
      and motion in the center of things—
except the man lives in dread
      of air   nature   life   guarded
by a blue surgeon's mask:
      the dance and what seems a blue
stub of a beak amaze the bird.
      He accepts me a moment when I stop,
opens and closes his beak,
      eyes fixed on the man, *quawks*
once hoarsely and lifts off
      across a narrow vein of water
and beats across the bay on wide wings.
      Is he a spirit who comes each dawn
to fill the beach with memories
      of past life and love
caught by the man until light
      and tourists gathering kill
the bareness needed for recall?
      Or is he Jeffer's spirit
not seamed in granite
      as that poet dreamed, but bound

in wing and feather to haunt
      his tragic shore now cheapened
by trinkets and coffee cups?
      The next day I come in his place:
I come and come but only
      rock and wave greet me until
one-legged I stare unmoving
      towards the shore, awaiting
another strangeness to meet my own
      and make a stranger harmony...

ORION SETTING

for Olga Carlisle

A week of fog, early for the season,
   one of our three: summer, rain,
the gray haven between.
   Tonight skies clear, and there
Orion falls into the western ocean
   who rose in the east with autumn.
Earlier our parrot flocks tore the sky
   with raucous cries:
a hawk's red tail flashed on and off
   in the silver light,
and a crow risked all harrying him
   from her young:
offshore, boats tracked herring
   while dolphins hunted the waves' edge
their fierceness at such distance
   part of the surf's appeal.
Even earlier our friend
   tried to draw the garden's calm
ripe from years coming to fullness,
   but what we want to paint or write
or catch from wind and wave
   cannot be caught, the peace
never the same however often
   we step in its flow,
puzzling in the way it balances
   so much desire and despair.
Look how the slow surge
   of the new leaves' green

swallows the plum's white blooms:
   feel the hawk in the heart
plummet from hunger.
   But when night wheels into morning,
the air invisibly littered with stars,
   suddenly it seems that all
that lives and dies is one great jewel
   we see face by face
so we say 'We are here' or 'This was done'
   or 'Evil won out there'
when we are all at one beneath
   the different faces we bear.

THE TRUE SELF IS NOT IN MOTION

When rain's marathon is run
a mist remains in a world
washed of color and shape:

to see a tree loom darkly
and then disappear as another
nearly finds its form

makes me ask if life and death
are only shades that fade
repeatedly into each other?

All too soon the sun imposes
the solid, certain world,
and years whose steps we climb

to keep the date
we made with death
when we were born.

Which is true? Earnest shifting,
hard certainties? Both, perhaps:
life is not simply run.

The true self is not in motion—
just its shadow is glimpsed
like a deer at rest

in dense, twilit woods.

ABOUT THE AUTHOR

Lance Lee is a poet, playwright, novelist (*Second Chances*) and writer on drama and screenwriting (*The Death and Life of Drama*). Previous volumes of poetry include *Wrestling With The Angel* and *Becoming Human*. His poems appear widely in this country and England, where half his family lives, and he is a past Creative Writing Fellow of the National Endowment for the Arts. His home is in Los Angeles, where he has taught in a number of universities, and was instrumental in forming the State Park system in the Santa Monica Mountains...

ABOUT THE BOOK

Human/Nature was set in 12 pt. Palatino on a Macintosh G4 by Pro•To•Type, Middletown, NY, and was printed and bound by Royal Fireworks Press, Unionville, NY. Birch Brook Press published this book at Delhi, NY.